Stephanie Thompson

The Taking **Responsibility** Programme

A primary school behaviour management programme that delivers results – fast!

PUPIL WORKSHEETS BOOK 2

Title:	The Taking Responsibility Programme Book 2: Pupil Worksheets
Author:	S. Thompson
Editors:	Marie Langley and Tanya Tremewan
Designer:	David Johnstone
Book code:	PB00122
ISBN:	978-1-908736-01-7
Published:	2012
Publisher:	TTS Group Ltd
	Park Lane Business Park Kirkby-in-Ashfield Notts, NG17 9GU Tel: 0800 318 686 Fax: 0800 137 525
Websites:	www.tts-shopping.com
Copyright:	Text: © S.Thompson, 2008 Edition and Illustrations: © TTS Group Ltd, 2012
About the author:	S. Thompson is headteacher of a semi-rural school in the South Island of New Zealand. She has been at her school since the beginning of 2002. During that time she has re-developed and instigated a number of new processes and systems at her school. Prior to her current position, she taught in a larger urban primary school. She has taught across all levels of the school and has been working in education for more than a decade.

Photocopy Notice:

Permission is given to schools and teachers who buy this book to reproduce it (and/or any extracts) by photocopying or otherwise, but only for use at their present school. Copies may not be supplied to anyone else or made or used for any other purpose.

Contents

Introduction   4
How TRP works   4
How to use the TRP worksheets   4

Common questions about TRP   5
    Taking Responsibility Programme pupil report sheet   6
    TRP points record   7

Worksheets
    Anger (1)   8
    Anger (2)   9
    Anger (3)   10
    Anger (4)   11
    Annoying others   12
    Bullying (1)   13
    Bullying (2)   14
    Bullying (3)   15
    Put downs   16
    Swearing (1)   17
    Swearing (2)   18
    Swearing again   19
    Spitting   20
    Taking things   21
    Unsporting behaviour   22
    Not listening   23
    Being disrespectful   24
    Being dishonest   25
    Learning from others   26
    Learning strategies   27
    Personal learning strategies   28
    Being a good friend   29
    Building a friendship   30
    What is a friend?   31
    Friends are a reflection of ourselves   32
    Friends as role models   33
    Friendship skills   34
    Saying "Sorry"   35
    Stress   36
    The nosey bird   37
    Attitudes to situations   38
    Building someone up   40
    GC and BC   41
    Relating to others   42
    The hornets' nest   43
    Thinking before speaking   44
    Bertie the Bus   45
    Pestery Pete   46
    Stress busters   47

Introduction

This book is a companion to *The Taking Responsibility Programme, Book 1: An Introduction to TRP*. Book 1 contains information about the philosophy and origins of the Taking Responsibility Programme (TRP) along with general information about introducing the TRP programme in your school. It also contains TRP worksheets that deal with issues at a fairly general level. Book 2 contains a selection of worksheets targeting more specific behaviours to be used as and when they are appropriate to your implementation of TRP.

How TRP works

It is important that, to begin with, school-wide expectations for behaviour inside and outside the classroom are made clear to all. Any pupils who fail to meet these expectations are then allocated a number of 'sad points'. Pupils are involved in determining the reasons for sad points and in deciding how many points any action warrants.

If pupils reach a predetermined number of points they need to participate in TRP. This programme is run by a staff member during break and lunchtime. (This will be a teacher on duty in most cases. The headteacher or a senior teacher is an effective person to have in charge of the programme overall.) The worksheets that form the basis of the TRP feature in this series.

After going through the programme, pupils are required to take home the 'Pupil report sheet' (page 6)(and on occasions the worksheet activities) to be signed. The sheet outlines why a pupil has had to take part in TRP, what they did and the alternative behaviour options.

How to use the TRP worksheets

The TRP worksheets can be used in a number of different ways. They can be used as:

- stand-alone worksheets
- discussion starters
- a 'Relationships' health programme
- a class climate unit
- a school-wide behaviour management programme
- a class programme
- a drama resource (instead of writing a response, pupils could use drama to explore situations and solutions).

Each worksheet includes a series of questions or statement starters that encourage the pupils to reflect on the behaviour which has brought them into TRP. In some cases the response can be through drawing a picture. Pupils are also encouraged to consider why they should and how they could avoid repeating the same unacceptable behaviour.

Common questions about TRP

Who uses TRP?

TRP can be used by anyone. It is most effective as a whole-school approach, but it can also be used by supply teachers, teacher assistants with small groups or class teachers. The worksheets and ideas have been designed for the primary school. They may be successfully adapted for use with older pupils; alternatively, see the two books in this series that have been specifically designed for implementing TRP with adolescents.

What do pupils do in TRP?

The activities involved in TRP will depend on why a given pupil is taking part. If, for example, a pupil has collected sad points for inappropriate behaviour in the classroom, the programme would cover aspects of how to take responsibility for behaviour, solutions to problems and self-esteem. If the pupil has come into the programme due to an action resulting from loss of self-control, the programme may include activities for controlling anger.

Why should we take on this programme in particular?

TRP was instigated on the grounds that it is important to sort out any issues as they arise. We believe in getting to the root of the problem and in helping pupils find out why something has happened and how to fix it.

Are pupils kept clearly informed about what is happening?

Pupils have clear guidelines about what is acceptable and what is not. They know in advance what behaviour is likely to earn them sad points. They also know – in fact they have helped to decide – how many points any action may cost them. At the end of the week, points are wiped, leaving pupils able to start afresh the following week.

What do we need to do to make TRP a success?

An important key to success is to be consistent. Work with pupils to negotiate sad points and inappropriate behaviours. If you do this, you will probably avoid the initial complaints and defiance that can come from pupils when they are introduced to something new. It is all about expectation: you expect the best from all pupils for all pupils, and this programme is for them to help them. The same applies to headteachers wishing to implement TRP as a whole-school approach: work with your staff to ensure full success.

TRP does work. More importantly, it helps pupils gain the skills and values they need. Kids are the way they are because of what adults do to them and around them. When we remember this, we are better able to help our pupils who struggle – they are struggling because they don't know differently yet. With your help, they soon will know better!

Taking Responsibility Programme pupil report sheet

School: _____ Date: _____

Pupil: _____

Dear Parent/Caregiver

Any pupil who does not abide by our school expectations is placed in the Taking Responsibility Programme (TRP). He or she is asked to reflect upon the reason for placement in the Taking Responsibility Programme and must write a plan for improving his or her behaviour. Please discuss this Taking Responsibility Programme report with your child, sign it, and return the report tomorrow. Your support is much appreciated.

Reason for placement in the Taking Responsibility Programme:

_____

_____

Days in the programme: _____

Plan for improving my behaviour by taking responsibility:

_____

_____

_____

What I worked on and learnt during the Taking Responsibility Programme:

_____

_____

_____

Parent comments:

_____

_____

_____

_____

Teacher comments:

_____

_____

_____

_____

Pupil signature:

_____

Parent signature:

_____

Teacher signature:

_____

TRP points record for Week

Name	Monday	Tuesday	Wednesday	Thursday	Friday	Total

Anger (1)

What does anger look like for you?

_____
_____

Draw a picture of you feeling angry. Label important parts of your picture.

[   ]

What happens to you when you get angry?

_____
_____

What makes you most angry?	How often do you get angry?

When was the last time you got angry?

_____
_____

What did you do to deal with it?

_____
_____

What are safe ways to get angry?

_____
_____

Anger (2)

Draw the angriest picture you can.

What is happening in your picture?

_____
_____
_____

What would make your picture happy? Draw the positive side.

_____
_____
_____

Anger (3)

What happened to make you angry enough to be in this programme?

_____
_____
_____

How did you feel when it happened?

_____
_____
_____

Who did you affect when you got angry?

_____
_____

How do you think the other people felt? List the emotions they may have had and why.

NAME	EMOTION	WHY
_____	_____	_____
_____	_____	_____

How do you feel about the way they may have felt and why?

_____
_____
_____

How could your actions have made someone feel positive instead of negative? (What could you have done instead?)

_____
_____
_____

Anger (4)

Different things make different people angry. These are called triggers. Everyone's anger triggers are different.

Write down what things trigger your anger.

1. _____

2. _____

3. _____

4. _____

What happens to you when you get angry?

_____

Write down what triggered you this time.

_____

How else could you have behaved when you felt angry this time?

_____

Annoying others

When I annoy others I do these things:

It makes me feel:

I annoy others for these reasons:

My teachers don't like it when I annoy others because:

My classmates don't like it when I annoy them because:

This is what I can do instead when I feel like annoying others:

Bullying (1)

Draw a picture of a bully.

Draw a picture of what happened to bring you into TRP.

Draw a picture of how the other person feels.

Draw a picture of how you feel now.

Draw a picture of how to solve this problem and what you would do next time.

Bullying (2)

What does a bully do?

Why are you in this programme?

Were your actions the actions of a bully? Why?

How do you feel about what happened?   How does the other person feel?

What could you have done differently?

What will you do next time?

Bullying (3)

What is bullying? (Fill in the gaps.)

Bullying is when someone keeps _____

or _____

or when they _____

I think bullying is also _____

Why do some people bully? (Unscramble the words.)

- To be pprlauro. _____
- To look ghtou. _____
- To get tttaenion or things. _____
- To make others aaridf of them. _____
- Or because they are being dieullb themselves. _____

Why do you think some people are bullied?

_____

_____

Do you think bullying is harmful? _____

Explain why you think this.

_____

_____

What can you do? I can _____

_____

An adult you can trust to talk about these issues might be (list 3)

1. _____

2. _____

3. _____

Put downs

A put down is:
_____
_____

What I said that put someone down, and the circumstances behind it:
_____
_____
_____

Why I said what I said:	I put others down because:
_____	_____
_____	_____
_____	_____

When I put someone down I feel:
_____
_____
_____

When I put someone down they would feel:
_____
_____
_____

Instead of putting someone down I could say:
_____
_____

Swearing (1)

I swear because:

When I swear I feel:

When I swear at someone they would feel:

Instead of swearing I could say these words:

Swearing (2)

I swore at these people:

_____

_____

_____

_____

I said:

_____

_____

_____

_____

I swore at them because:

_____

_____

_____

_____

This was unacceptable because:

_____

_____

_____

_____

I can make amends to these people by:

_____

_____

_____

_____

Swearing again

I have had to join the programme for swearing more than once.

When I swear at someone, the other person feels:

_____
_____
_____
_____

When I swear the adults feel:

_____
_____
_____
_____

I notice that I swear during these times:

_____
_____
_____
_____

Instead of swearing, I need to look at other ways to control my behaviour such as:

_____
_____
_____
_____

Spitting

What happened?

_____
_____
_____

Why did I spit?

_____
_____
_____
_____

I felt:

_____
_____
_____
_____

The other person would have felt:

_____
_____
_____

Spitting was an inappropriate choice because:

_____
_____
_____
_____

This is what I could have done instead:

_____
_____
_____
_____

Taking things

What happened?

What did you take?

Why?

How did you feel when this happened?

How do you think the owner felt?

What can you do to make amends?

Unsporting behaviour

This is what I did that was unsporting:

I did this because:

The other/s in my game would have felt:

This is what I would do next time:

These people are great role models of good sportsmanship:

If they knew I was being unfair they would think:

How I feel about it now:

Not listening

This is a picture of me listening.

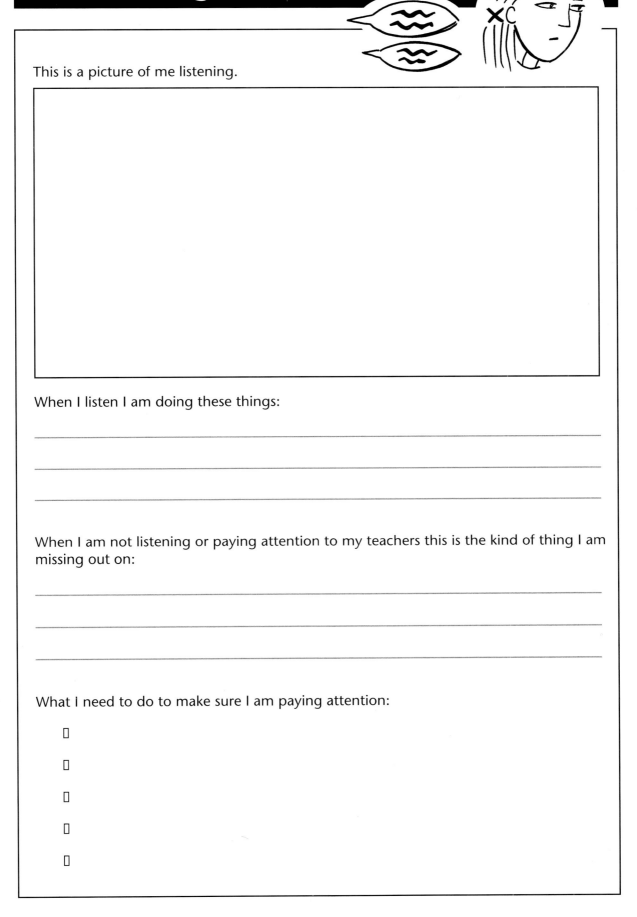

When I listen I am doing these things:

_____
_____
_____

When I am not listening or paying attention to my teachers this is the kind of thing I am missing out on:

_____
_____
_____

What I need to do to make sure I am paying attention:

- ☐
- ☐
- ☐
- ☐
- ☐

Being disrespectful

This is what I was doing that is considered disrespectful:

_____

This is why my behaviour was considered disrespectful:

_____

This is a better way of dealing with the situation:

_____

This is what I need to do to have self-control of my behaviour:

_____

This is a picture of me having self control in a similar situation:

Being dishonest

What does it mean to 'be honest'?

___

Why should people be honest?

___

Think of someone you know and like who you think is honest.

Write down their name. ___

Why do you think they are honest? Describe what they do.

___

Think of a time when you have been honest – describe what it was like, what happened and how you felt.

___

What is the difference in being honest and dishonest? Explain what each one feels like.

Honest feels: ___

Dishonest feels: ___

I prefer ___ because ___

Learning from others

Name a person you admire:
Classmate:

Other:

What is it about them that you admire?

What do they do that makes them a good role model? (Think about their behaviour and the way they take responsibility.)

Classmate:

Other:

What qualities do you have in common with this person?

Classmate:

Other:

What would you like to learn from them in terms of their good qualities?

Classmate:

Other:

How will you make this happen?

Learning strategies

What are learning strategies?

_____

_____

_____

Why do we need learning strategies?

_____

_____

_____

Who uses them?

_____

_____

List as many learning strategies as you can think of and when and why you use them.

Strategy:	When you use it:	What you use it for:

Personal learning strategies

What learning strategies do you know?

_____
_____
_____

What other strategies do you think you could benefit from?

_____
_____
_____

Who do you know who has good strategies and why do you think so?

Person: _____

Why I think this person has good learning strategies:

_____
_____

What is your plan of action so that you can improve your learning strategies?

What I need to do:

_____
_____
_____

Who can help me:

_____

Being a good friend

Being a good friend is important to me because:

_____
_____
_____

I am a good friend because:

_____
_____
_____

I could help other people be a good friend by:

_____
_____
_____

If I could describe what a good friend is like I would say a good friend:

Looks like …	Sounds like …	Does these things …
_____	_____	_____
_____	_____	_____
_____	_____	_____
_____	_____	_____
_____	_____	_____
_____	_____	_____

Building a friendship

Why do we need friends?

_____

_____

_____

Who are your friends?

_____   _____

_____   _____

_____   _____

Why do you like being with your friends?

_____

_____

_____

_____

What do they do that makes you feel great hanging around with them?

_____

_____

_____

What are your favourite things to do with your friends?

_____

_____

_____

What do you do to help your friendships stay strong?

_____

_____

_____

Imagine you are the world's expert in friends. What ideas and tips would you give people on how to be a good friend? Make a list of these ideas. You could produce a poster/write them down or draw them. (Think about how you treat friends when they are hurt, how you share toys/games and ideas, how you introduce them to others ...)

What is a friend?

What kinds of qualities does a good friend have?

_____   _____

_____   _____

_____   _____

What kinds of qualities do you have, that make you a good friend?

What kinds of things do you think you could work on to be an even better friend?

_____   _____

_____   _____

_____   _____

Draw a picture or write a story/poem/quote that shows the qualities you and your friends have.

Friends are a reflection of ourselves

What does it mean, "friends are a reflection of ourselves"?
_____
_____
_____

What do you do if your friends hurt themselves?
_____
_____

Explain how you treat your friends when you are playing in the playground.
_____
_____

What do you do if your friend does not listen to you?
_____
_____

Think of your friends: who does most of the talking?
_____

When you are playing with your friends, who thinks of the game to play?
_____

What happens if you don't play the game mentioned above?
_____
_____

What have you learnt about you and your friends from doing this?
_____
_____
_____

Friends as role models

Think of someone who is a good friend of yours.

Name: _____

What do they do that makes them a good friend?

_____
_____

Describe a situation where they were a good friend.

_____
_____
_____

What sort of skills do they use?

_____
_____
_____

Why do you like being with them?

_____
_____
_____

What could you do to be more like them?

_____
_____
_____

If you were more like them, what changes would that mean for you? How would you be different?

_____
_____

Friendship skills

What do you think are the four most important skills someone needs to be a good friend?

_____   _____

_____   _____

Why?

_____

_____

_____

What are the best skills your friends have?

_____   _____

_____   _____

Why do you think this?

_____

_____

How do they show these skills?

_____

_____

Thinking about yourself, what would be a good skill for you to learn that you DON'T already have?

_____

Why?

_____

_____

_____

Plan out how you will learn this skill, who from, and how you will use it to improve your friendships.

_____

_____

_____

Saying "Sorry!"

Sometimes a really good apology can make the world of difference when something goes wrong. This is especially true if you make a mistake or if what has happened is an accident. There are different ways to apologise.

Write a list of things you can do to apologise.

_____

_____

_____

Write a list of ways to say "Sorry".

_____

_____

_____

Why is it important to apologise when there is a mishap?

_____

_____

Should you apologise if you think you are not wrong?

_____

Draw a picture or write a story/poem/quote about what the other person feels like when they get a heartfelt apology.

Stress

What do you think stress is?

_____
_____
_____

Why?

_____
_____

What does stress …

look like:	sound like:	feel like:

What caused you to feel stressed-out?

_____

Do you have any control over stressful situations?

_____

Why/how?

_____
_____

What could you do to have more control over feeling stressed?

_____
_____

© TTS Group Ltd, 2012

The nosey bird

Ori the Ostrich was a nosey bird. He just could not help poking his nose into everyone else's problems and business. As you can imagine, this did not make him a very popular bird! Everyone told him "It may be of interest to you but it is not your concern! Keep your beak out of it!"

Your job is to help Ori become a better bird friend for everyone!

What sort of behaviours do you think Ori had when he was being nosey?

_____
_____
_____

Why do you think Ori could do with some new behaviours?

_____
_____
_____

What new behaviours do you think Ori should learn so that he is no longer seen as a nosey bird?

_____
_____
_____

In what way do you think Ori's relationships with his bird friends will change if he can stop being nosey?

_____
_____
_____

Attitudes to situations

Andy the Aardvark was an interesting creature. Sometimes he had a problem adjusting his attitude to a situation to make things go better for him. As you can imagine, this often caused frustration for those around him and made the situation for Andy a lot worse than it needed to be.

Your job is to help Andy the Aardvark work on his attitude so that when he is faced with a difficult situation, instead of making the situation worse, things work out much better for everyone.

What is an attitude? Draw or write down what you think it is.

Write down what you think "attitude" is.

A good attitude ...

looks like:	sounds like:

© TTS Group Ltd, 2012

A bad attitude ...

looks like:	sounds like:

What kind of attitude do you think Andy had? Why?

Describe several situations where Andy's attitude would make the situation worse.

Explain why you think Andy's attitude needs adjusting.

What would you suggest to Andy to help him with adjusting his attitude?

If he worked on it, what would the outcome be? How will others view him then?

What advice would you give Andy that you know would work and make the situation better?

Building someone up

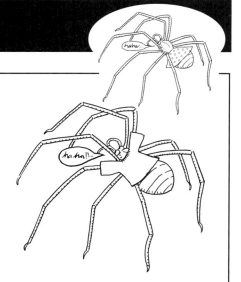

Sarah and Sam were spiders and they had been friends for a long time. Unfortunately they did not always act like it. Sometimes, one of them made fun of the other, in front of classmates, trying to make herself or himself look good at the expense of the other friend. This was a real shame, because both spiders were good at heart. But they didn't realise that what they were doing was hurting one another. Oh, what a tangled web of trouble they had woven for themselves!

What does this mean: "Making yourself look good at the expense of your friends"?

_____

_____

Write down an example of this happening. (It could be a real example or one you have made up.)

_____

_____

When one of the spider friends did this to the other, how do you think it made the other friend feel?

_____

_____

What do you think are the feelings of the person who is making himself or herself look good at the friend's expense? Explain why you think they do this.

_____

_____

What would you suggest to both Sam and Sarah that would help them? Suggest some strategies that would "build up" friends, not "bring them down".

_____

_____

_____

_____

GC and BC

At Ant-icipation School, there were two classes who had a mix of fabulous pupil ants. In the GC class, the ant pupils were very good at making good choices. In the BC class, the ant pupils had difficulty making sensible decisions and always seemed to make bad choices. As you can imagine, the BC class was worrying all the teachers, and they did not know what to do about it.

They need your help!!

What sorts of behaviours did the GC ant pupils have when they needed to make a decision?

_____
_____
_____
_____
_____

What sorts of behaviours did the BC ant pupils have when they needed to make a decision?

_____
_____
_____
_____
_____

Which class of ants achieved higher quality work and had better relationships with their teachers and peers? Why?

_____
_____
_____

If you were in a school where some pupils were unable to make a Good Choice (GC), what would you suggest they could do?

_____
_____
_____
_____
_____

Relating to others

Deirdre the Duck was having a difficult time at school. No matter how hard she tried, she just couldn't help getting into trouble with her classmates – she seemed to be constantly bickering with them. Not only was this frustrating for her, but it was worrying for both her teachers and her parents. Her classmates were sick of it and this made it difficult for her to make good friends.

What could she do about it?

_____

_____

What sort of behaviour was Deirdre displaying that made life more difficult than it needed to be?

_____

_____

If you were Deirdre's friend (or teacher or parent), what suggestions would you give her to help improve her relationships with her classmates?

_____

_____

What kind of action plan could Deirdre put in place that would help her relate to her classmates and make good friends? Write the plan out in steps.

Step one:	Step two:

Step three:	Step four:

The hornets' nest

Harry and Harriet were hornets. They lived in a large nest with many other hornets. As you can imagine, in a community like that, it was essential for them to all get along. They didn't always have to be friends, but they needed to work together to get things done and cause minimum trouble. Unfortunately, Harry and Harriet had difficulty working with the other hornets. They did not seem to have the skills to relate to others, and often used the sting in their tails to "stir up" a frenzy.

What a shame for them both! What do you think could be done to help them become better members of their community?

What kinds of behaviour did Harry and Harriet have that "stirred up" the other hornets?

_____
_____

Why do you think both of them acted this way?

_____
_____
_____

Explain how you think the other community members would feel.

_____
_____
_____

What would you advise Harry and Harriet to do in order to relate better with the other hornets?

_____
_____
_____

How would this advice change Harry and Harriet's behaviour and their relationships with others?

_____
_____
_____

Thinking before speaking

Goosey the Gander was having trouble at school. Although Goosey was a friendly, bright pupil, sometimes he got into a spot of bother with his geese classmates. For some reason, he felt his ideas were the best, and his opinion was the most important – so much so that it was impossible for other geese to express their own ideas or even get a hiss or a honk in edgeways!

Oh dear, what could be done about it? He needs your help!

Describe what Goosey was doing to upset his geese classmates.

_____

_____

_____

Why do you think Goosey acted this way?

_____

_____

_____

Explain how you think his classmates felt.

_____

_____

_____

What would you advise Goosey to do in order to relate better with his classmates?

_____

_____

_____

How would this advice change Goosey's behaviour and his relationships with others?

_____

_____

_____

Bertie the Bus

Bertie the Bus was getting cross! Usually, he loved being a school bus: the children talked about interesting subjects and he often learnt many new things. Most of the time the children were kind to him, treating him with respect, but lately, there had been a small group of pupils who were being quite rude. Not only were they being cheeky to the poor bus driver, but they were making Bertie messy! Bertie hated being messy – bits of paper rubbish wasn't so bad, but the food – YUCK! What do you think he could do about it?

What sorts of things did the children do that made Bertie cross?

_____
_____
_____

Explain what you would do if you were Bertie.

_____
_____
_____

Write down a list of common-sense things that the children should do on the bus to make Bertie much happier.

_____
_____
_____
_____
_____

Pestery Pete

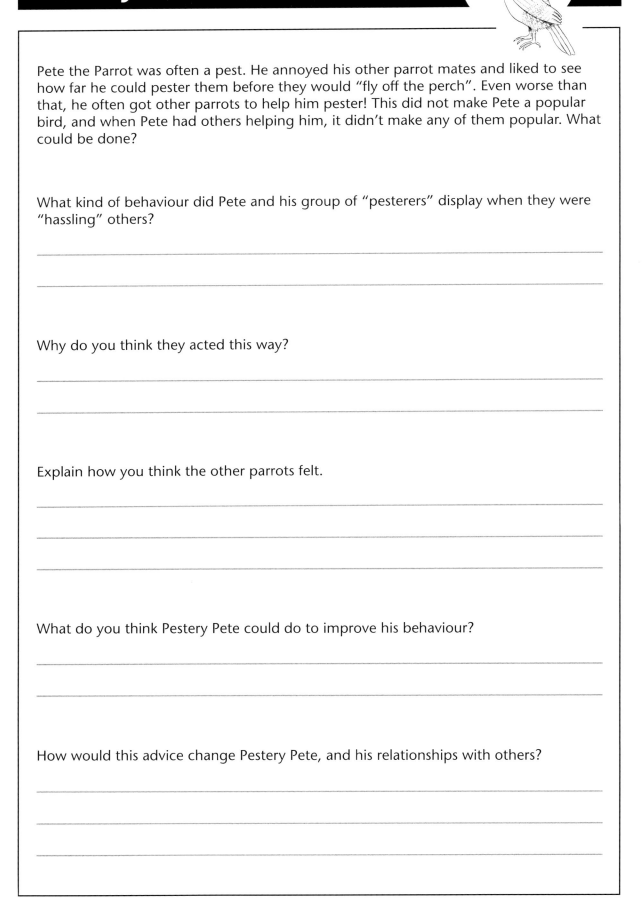

Pete the Parrot was often a pest. He annoyed his other parrot mates and liked to see how far he could pester them before they would "fly off the perch". Even worse than that, he often got other parrots to help him pester! This did not make Pete a popular bird, and when Pete had others helping him, it didn't make any of them popular. What could be done?

What kind of behaviour did Pete and his group of "pesterers" display when they were "hassling" others?

_____
_____

Why do you think they acted this way?

_____
_____

Explain how you think the other parrots felt.

_____
_____
_____

What do you think Pestery Pete could do to improve his behaviour?

_____
_____

How would this advice change Pestery Pete, and his relationships with others?

_____
_____
_____

Stress busters

Lacana the lioness cub was feeling stressed out. Her homework was due and she had been so busy in the den with all the things happening during the week – cub-nastics, hunt camp, and claw sharpening lessons – that she hadn't even started working on it! She kept thinking "Oh my goodness, you are soooo in trouble! Your teacher will nag and Mum and Dad will be sooo angry …" The more she "thought talked" (you know, where you talk to yourself in your mind), the more stressed out she became. Lacana needed help fast!

Every now and then we find ourselves in stressful situations like Lacana or simply feel a little stressed out. Being in control of the feelings we have when we are stressed out can be really difficult and sometimes it is good to have strategies that help us. Perhaps you can think of some strategies (ideas) that could help Lacana.

What was the situation that had Lacana stressed out?

___

What other "thought talk" might she have?

___

How was Lacana feeling about this?

___

Describe a situation that stresses you out.

___

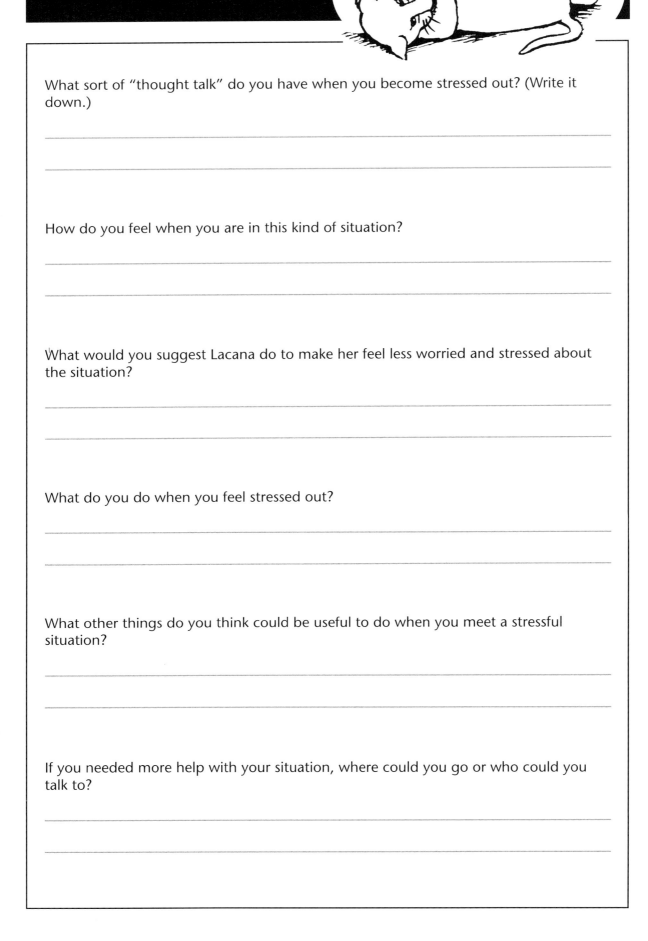

What sort of "thought talk" do you have when you become stressed out? (Write it down.)

How do you feel when you are in this kind of situation?

What would you suggest Lacana do to make her feel less worried and stressed about the situation?

What do you do when you feel stressed out?

What other things do you think could be useful to do when you meet a stressful situation?

If you needed more help with your situation, where could you go or who could you talk to?